SCHIRMER'S LIBRARY
OF MUSICAL CLASSICS

Vol. 700

HUGO REINHOLD

Op. 39

Miniatures

Twenty-Four
Short and Easy Piano-Pieces for
the Development of Musical Style

Edited and Fingered by
LOUIS OESTERLE

ISBN 978-0-7935-7285-4

G. SCHIRMER, Inc.

DISTRIBUTED BY

HAL•LEONARD®
CORPORATION
7777 W. BLUEMOUND RD. P.O. BOX 13819 MILWAUKEE, WI 53213

CONTENTS

Miniaturbilder.
Miniatures.
Marsch.
March.

Nicht zu schnell und sehr rhythmisch.
Allegro non troppo e ben ritmato.

HUGO REINHOLD. Op. 39.

Märchenbild.
Fairy Tale.

Étude.

Ziemlich schnell.
Allegro non troppo.

Walzer.
Waltz.

Savoyardenknabe.

Savoyard Boy.

Mässig, doch nicht schleppend.

Moderato ma non strascinando.

8

Scherzo.

Dudelsackpfeifer.
The Bagpipe.

Ziemlich schnell.
Allegro non troppo.

Ständchen.
Serenade.

Getragen.
Sostenuto.

8.

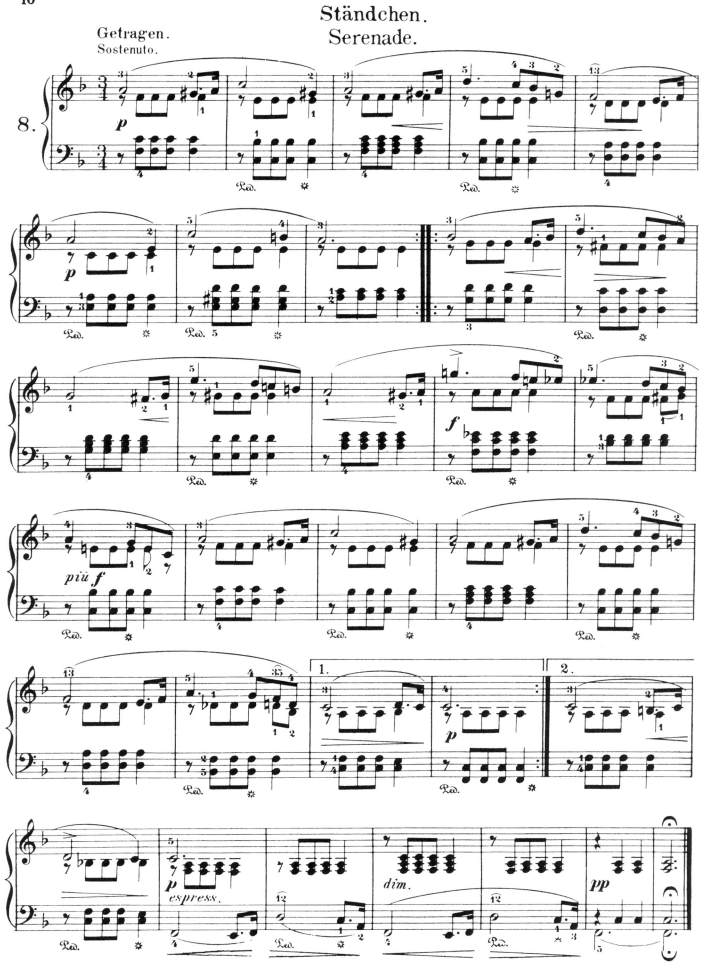

Ungarisch.
Hungarian Dance.

In der Schule.
At School.

Humoreske.

Leicht bewegt.
Leggero con moto.

11.

Silhouette.

Zigeunerlied.
Gypsy-song.

Hugo Reinhold, Op. 39, No. 13

Jagd-Fanfare.
Hunter's Call.

Arietta.

Schlummerlied.
Slumber-song.

Getragen.
Sostenuto.

16.

Kriegslied.
War-song.

17.

Geständniss.
Confession.

18.

Gondoliera.

Nachtstück.
Nocturne.

Abgemessen, doch nicht schleppend.
Misurato ma non strascinando.

Intermezzo.

21.

Mélancolie.
Melancholy.

Getragen, doch nicht schleppend.
Sostenuto ma non strascinando.

22.

Papillon.
Butterfly.

Russisch.
Russian Dance.

Möglichst rasch.
Allegro assai.

24.